BE STRONG

THE RISE OF BELOVED PUBLIC ART SCULPTOR NANCY SCHÖN

WRITTEN BY
DARCY PATTISON

ILLUSTRATED BY
RICH DAVIS

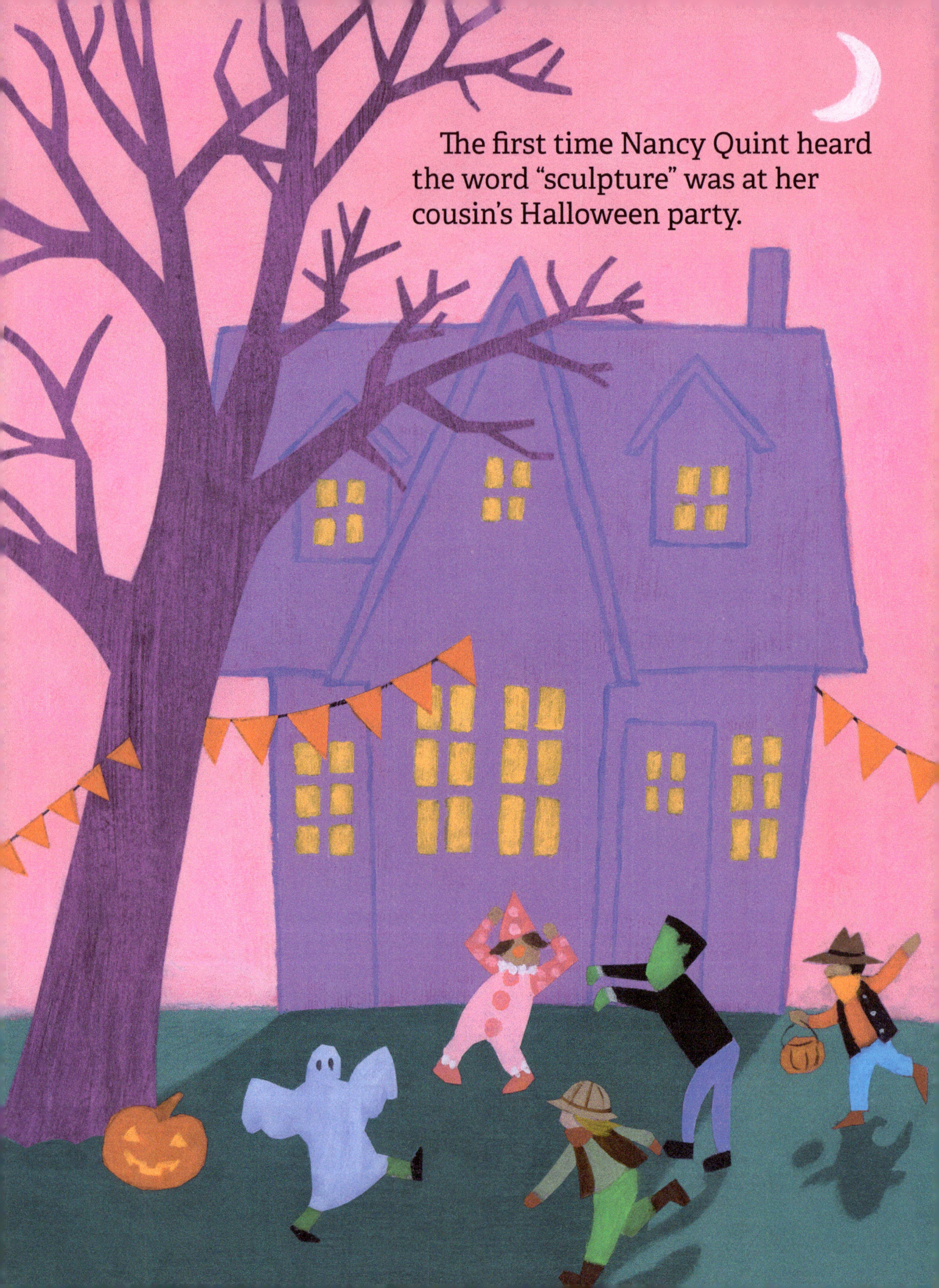

The first time Nancy Quint heard the word "sculpture" was at her cousin's Halloween party.

For one game, each child was asked to chew a piece of gum and use it to sculpt something.
Her hands shaped a tiny cup and saucer.

She won first place!

SCULPTURE!

Nancy graduated from the School of the Museum of Fine Arts, Boston, with a degree in sculpture.

She married and became Nancy Schön. Like many women, she chose to raise a family.

During those years, she taught art and made sculptures of mothers and children. Just small pieces. Nothing big.

Then, on a sunny day in 1979, Nancy strolled through a garden of bronze sculptures. In one sculpture, a bronze woman cuddled a bronze cat. When children walked past the sculpture...

...they patted the cat.

Or tickled it.

Or talked to it.
And no one stopped them!

Later, Nancy wrote,

*"Right then, I saw what I wanted for my art.
I wanted my sculptures
to be outdoors in parks,
where people of all ages
could touch
and enjoy them."*

MACK — Terrible pose!

NACK — Fix the lid on the eye.

PACK — Pull up the feathers for a bit of action.

OUACK — Tilt the head back more.

QUACK — What might cause a child to fall in love with this duck?

One day, Nancy sat in her studio, tired and discouraged. So many problems!

Would she ever get the ducklings right?

The artist whose studio was across the hall stopped to talk. "What's wrong?" she asked.

Nancy explained the problems.

The artist disappeared but came back and handed Nancy a piece of paper with two words:

BE STRONG!

That encouragement was just what Nancy needed.
She got back to work.

The duck sculptures were based on Robert McCloskey's popular book *Make Way for Ducklings*.

But would the author be pleased with the duck family?

When he came to check on the sculpture's progress, *he said, "They might be too large."*

Be strong!
Nancy reminded herself.

She knew that when you move a large sculpture from the studio to outside, it seems smaller. Nancy and her friend hoisted Mrs. Mallard and three ducklings onto dollies and rolled them outside.

A mother and three kids came walking by. The children ran to the ducklings and patted their heads.
They asked, "Can we sit on the ducks?"

The duck family was kid-perfect!
It was a magical moment for the author and the sculptor.

In 1987, on a rainy October day—perfect weather for ducks—the duck family went to live in Boston's Public Garden, a beautiful park.

Kids ran to the ducks to pet, climb, hug, feed, or talk to them. Nancy was thrilled. It was the beginning of a career in public art.

A lifelong fan of the Boston Marathon, Nancy decided to create a public art sculpture about the race. She chose Aesop's fable "The Tortoise and the Hare" as a way to honor everyone who ran.

Fast. Or s-l-o-w.

But public art is expensive and takes a long time. On hard days, Nancy reminded herself,

BE STRONG!

Finally, after seven long years, *Tortoise and Hare* was installed in Copley Square, the finish line of the Boston Marathon.

Nancy wrote:

"I had put a smile on the tortoise's face. Now, as young and old walked by, I saw them smiling back."

Over the years, Nancy has created dozens of public art sculptures.
 Around the nation,
  in outdoor parks,

with raccoons,

children now run

slip over

and under

and around prairie dogs,

comfort Eeyore with a hug,

pat Pooh Bear's belly,

listen to Piglet's stories,

rub a dragon's gem for luck and better grades,

and ride and dream

on the back
of a comfortable bronze caterpillar.

Making public art is hard.

Nancy wrote:

You shape an idea,
throw it away,
shrug, and start again.

Take away some, add.
Take away more.

You don't mind
(not too much)
because little by little
it gets better.

You keep at it,
you get help,
try again and again,
and then it works.

And on those hard days, Nancy always found in her heart and on her lips those two words:

BE STRONG!

THE RISE OF PUBLIC ART SCULPTOR NANCY SCHÖN

c. 1938. Nancy Quint as a child. *Unknown photographer.*

c. 1975. Before the *Make Way for Ducklings* sculpture, Nancy Schön was identified as simply an artist, not a public art sculptor. *Used with permission from the collections of the Newton Free Library, Newton, MA.*

ABOVE: c. 1987. Nancy Schön working on the ducklings sculpture in her studio. *Photo © David Wurzel.*

LEFT: c. 1987. Nancy Schön working on the ducklings sculpture. Notice the "Be Strong" sign on the wall behind her. *Photo © David Wurzel.*

May 13, 2019. Nancy Schön in the Myrtle Street Playground, Beacon Hill, Boston, MA. *Photo © John David Corey.*

2022. Nancy Schön and her grandchildren. *Photo © Jackie Schön.*
Front row, left to right: Natalie, Julia, Charlie
Middle row, left to right: Ben, Zeke, Nancy, Mia, Hannah
Top row, left to right: Jackie, Claire, David, Sivan

NANCY QUINT SCHÖN (1928)

c. 1995. Nancy Schön in her studio with the Hare sculpture. *Photo © David Wurzel.*

Nancy Quint Schön, an American sculptor, grew up near Boston, Massachusetts where her father ran his own florist shop. There, she learned to work hard and how to finish a job. At the School of the Museum of Fine Arts, she learned to sculpt. She married Donald Schön (1930-1997) and spent the next three decades raising their family of four children. In 1979, Nancy visited Mizpor Shalom sculpture garden in Ein Hod, Israel, which is devoted to the work of sculptor Ursula Malbin. It was there that Nancy saw the sculpture with the cat that encouraged her to pursue public art.

At the age of 59, her first public sculpture was installed in Boston's Public Garden, Boston, MA. The *Make Way for Ducklings* sculpture of a mother duck and her eight ducklings has become an iconic landmark. When First Lady Barbara Bush asked for a duplicate sculpture for Russian First Lady Raisa Gorbachev, Nancy and her crew flew to Moscow for the installation. Over the next three decades, Nancy has created over twenty public art installations that give children a place to play and interact with public art.

Nancy is now making some of the most complicated sculptures of her life. The process is streamlined by technology. She now sculpts the miniature of a sculpture, called a maquette. When it's approved, she has it scanned, and 3D printed at full size. She uses that as the armature, or framework, to create the final sculpture.

MAKE WAY FOR DUCKLINGS by Robert McCloskey

Nancy Schön's first public sculpture was based on Robert McCloskey's book, *Make Way for Ducklings*, which won the 1942 Caldecott Award, given by the American Library Association to the artist of the most distinguished American picture book for children. Robert McCloskey saw Nancy's drawings, the maquette (miniature sculpture, an early stage of the process) and the final sculptures. He approved of them all! From idea to installation, the *Make Way for Duckling* sculptures took two years. Most of Nancy's public art projects took years to complete.

A bronze plaque reads:

FOR THE CHILD IN ALL OF US

"CATERPILLAR"
Bronze sculpture created by Nancy Schön
2022

Photo © Nancy Schön

PUBLIC ART SCULPTURES BY NANCY SCHÖN

Over the years, Nancy Schön was asked to create large sculptures to be displayed in public areas. Each time, she had to receive approvals and find funding. Once, the funding was promised but then fell through, and she sold T-shirts to pay the costs. Another time, a committee took Nancy on an emotional ride by saying yes, then no, and then finally, yes. Several statues were commissioned by grieving families who had lost a loved one. Nancy's work helped them find a note of hope. Because public art is created for and installed in public places, an artist must always find advocates and supporters. It's never easy to create public art, but over and over, Nancy has found a way through resilience, stubbornness, determination, hope, and a lot of hard work.

- 1987 *Make Way for Ducklings,* Boston Public Garden, Boston, MA.
- 1991 *Make Way for Ducklings,* Novodevichy Park, Moscow, Russia.
- 1991 *Eeyore,* Children's Patio, Newton Free Library, Newton, MA
- 1995 *Tortoise and Hare,* Copley Square, Boston, MA.
- 1995 *Raccoons and the Magic Horseshoes,* Children's Bridge, Belle Meade, TN
- 1996 *Empty Sled and Dog, Sarah Pryor Memorial,* Hannah Williams Park, Wayland, MA
- 2000 *Dancing Girl,* Edmond and Lily Safra Children's Hospital, Tel Aviv, Israel
- 2001 *Winnie the Pooh and the Hunny Pot,* Children's Patio, Newton Free Library, Newton, MA
- 2002 *Lentil and his Dog,* Lentil Park, Hamilton, Ohio.
- 2002 *Gateway to Independence,* Carroll Center for the Blind, Newton, MA
- 2003 *Scholarly, Whimsical, Gentle, Lucky, and Loving Dragon,* Cambier Park, Naples, FL
- 2003 *A Dragon for Dorchester,* Nonquit Street Green, Dorchester, MA
- 2004 *Nursing Sundial,* Massachusetts General Hospital, Boston, MA
- 2008 *Butterflies in the Francis Street Garden,* Francis Street Garden, Boston, MA
- 2009 *Tortoise and Hare,* Crystal Bridges Museum of American Art, Bentonville, AR
- 2010 *Sal's Bear,* Children's Garden, Coastal Maine Botanical Gardens, Boothbay, ME
- 2012 *Piglet,* Children's Patio, Newton Free Library, Newton, MA
- 2014 *Friendship,* Children's Garden, Myriad Botanical Gardens, Oklahoma City, OK
- 2017 *Butterfly.* "Metamorphosis" exhibit at Regis College, Weston, MA
- 2019 *Myrtle the Turtle,* Myrtle Street Playground, Beacon Hill, MA
- 2021 *Diversity - The Owl and the Pussy Cat,* Nonquit Street Garden, Dorchester, MA
- 2021 *Newton Bronze Flower,* Newton Public Library, Newton MA
- 2022 *Caterpillar,* Waban Commons, Newton, MA
- 2022 *Charlie the Snail,* Boston Children's Hospital, Boston, MA
- 2022 *Millie the Ducky in a Puddle,* Concord Library, Concord, MA
- 2023 *"REACH" for Knowledge.* Wellesley Free Library, Wellesley MA
- Forthcoming. *Dialogue,* Two figures, Fu Jen University, New Taipei City, Taiwan
- Forthcoming. *Memorial for Italian immigrants,* Peace Garden of St. Leonard Church, Boston, MA

ABOVE: Nancy Schön working in her studio on May 30, 2023. Notice the "Be Strong" sign behind her. *Photo © Jackie Schön.*

BE STRONG: The Rise of Beloved Public Art Sculptor Nancy Schön
by Darcy Pattison
illustrated by Rich Davis

Text © 2024 Darcy Pattison
Illustrations © 2024 Rich Davis

Mims House
1309 Broadway
Little Rock, AR 72202
USA

MimsHouseBooks.com

Publisher's Cataloging-in-Publication data

Names: Pattison, Darcy, author. | Davis, Rich, 1958-, illustrator.
Title: Be strong : the rise of beloved public art sculptor Nancy Schön / written by Darcy Pattison; illustrated by Rich Davis.
Description: Little Rock, AR: Mims House, 2023. | Summary: The inspiring career of public art sculptor Nancy Schön, who learned to "Be Strong" as she worked on her sculptures.
Identifiers: LCCN: 2023910180 | ISBN: 9781629442365 (hardcover) | 9781629442372 (paperback) | 9781629442389 (ebook) | 9781629442396 (audio)
Subjects: LCSH Schön, Nancy, 1928- --Juvenile literature. | Sculptors--United States--Biography--Juvenile literature. | Artists--United States--Biography--Juvenile literature. | Women sculptors--United States--Biography--Juvenile literature. | Public sculpture--United States--Juvenile literature. | BISAC JUVENILE NONFICTION / Biography & Autobiography / Women | JUVENILE NONFICTION / Biography & Autobiography / Art | JUVENILE NONFICTION / Social Topics / Self-Esteem & Self-Reliance
Classification: LCC NB237.S377 .P38 Be 2023 | DDC 730.92--dc23

SOURCES
Interview with Nancy Schön by the author, July 2022.
Multiple conversations by video and email between Nancy Schön and the author, 2022–2023.
Schön, Nancy. *Make Way for Nancy: A Life in Public Art.* Boston: David R. Godine. 2017.

NOTE: When text is shown in *purple italics*, these are direct quotes–Nancy's thoughts and words–from this book: Schön, Nancy. *Make Way for Nancy: A Life in Public Art.* Boston: David R. Godine. 2017. Used with permission.

www.ingramcontent.com/pod-product-compliance
Lightning Source LLC
LaVergne TN
LVHW072053060526
838200LV00061B/4728